T0208336

GIRL TALK, MONEY TALK II

Financially Fit and Fabulous in Your 40s and 50s

LISA L. BROWN, CFP®, CIMA®, MBA

authorHOUSE®

AuthorHouse™
1663 Liberty Drive
Bloomington, IN 47403
www.authorhouse.com
Phone: 833-262-8899

Published by AuthorHouse 07/08/2021

ISBN: 978-1-6655-2744-6 (sc)
ISBN: 978-1-6655-2742-2 (hc)
ISBN: 978-1-6655-2743-9 (e)

Library of Congress Control Number: 2021910874

CONTENTS

PREFACE

Why This Book Matters and How It Will Help You

Many people really start focusing on their money in their forties and fifties to determine whether they are in good shape financially or need to make any changes. Sometimes this financial temperature taking is thrust upon them due to a sudden life change or major personal decision. Once they've begun the process of really paying attention to their money, they often say, "I wish I had done this years ago." Being financially aware and having a plan can bring so much clarity and peace of mind—in addition to minimizing fights about money if you are married.

Financially Fit and Fabulous in Your Forties and Fifties is the second book in my Girl Talk, Money Talk series. In 2019, I published the first book, *Girl Talk, Money Talk: The Smart Girl's Guide to Money After College*, giving young women in their twenties and thirties the basic financial knowledge to start life on solid footing. While I have written financial articles for more than a decade and have been published numerous times in prestigious publications including the *New York Times*, the *Wall Street Journal, Yahoo! Finance CNBC.com*, and *Kiplinger*, I didn't have a desire to write an entire book, or a book series, until a few years ago.

As a financial advisor, I started seeing a concerning trend of women in their forties and fifties being paralyzed from making any financial decisions. Phone calls were coming in from single women who needed to schedule an initial appointment with me, urgently. They'd come into my office and tell me their stories. The tales were similar. She was recently divorced or her husband just died, but either way, he had left her a pile of money (some piles larger than others). She needed help. These women all shared that they were never taught basic money management lessons and had been content allowing Daddy and then Husband handle the financial matters up to this point in their lives. These women

- had no idea what their monthly expenses were;
- were unsure whether this pile of money was going to be enough to take care of them and possibly their children too;
- questioned if they could stay in their house;
- worried they had to go get a job after being jobless for more than twenty years; and
- asked if they were destined to be a bag lady.

While these concerns are valid if you don't have a financial plan, the disturbing part to me was they had never been fully responsible for their own money. My heart went out to these women, and I became more convinced than ever that financial education must improve, especially for women.

It doesn't matter whether you came from money, grew up scraping by, or are a man or a woman. You need to understand your money situation—even if your spouse or significant other takes the main responsibility for it. Through my volunteer work in my community, supporting homeless families with children, I've seen college-educated women go from stable careers with roofs over their heads and food on the table to being homeless because they lacked basic money skills. Yes, financial disaster can even happen to smart women.

Here are some startling statistics:

- Sixty percent of women worry about not having enough money through retirement, citing lack of financial knowledge and experience as leading reasons.[1]
- While 53 percent of women are likely to talk with their partner about shopping tips, only 35 percent will talk about investments.[1]
- Nearly 60 percent of widows and divorcees say they wished they had been more involved in long-term financial decisions, and 74 percent don't consider themselves knowledgeable about investing. Ninety-eight percent of these women surveyed urge other women to become more involved with their finances early on.[2]

Women must not wait to manage money. It needs to happen now.

According to a 2020 white paper by consulting firm McKinsey, by 2030 American women are expected to control much of the $30 trillion in financial assets that baby boomers will possess.[3] This is close to the entire annual gross domestic product (GDP) of the United States.

Before you start reading this book, if you feel totally clueless about money, I encourage you to put down this book and pick up my first book, *Girl Talk, Money Talk: The Smart Girl's Guide to Money After College* (www.girltalkmoneytalk.com). There are many layers to a financial education, and my first book lays out the basic financial elements you'll need to digest the book in your hands now.

By writing a financial book series, my goal is to help you understand the impact money can have throughout your personal life. It's huge. I want you to have a solid understanding of what it takes now, in your forties and fifties, to become or remain financially stable and successful. As you are navigating the middle part of your life, this is also the time where new money opportunities, challenges, and decisions need to be addressed that were inconceivable one or two decades ago. Let's get you prepared. I never want you to feel you're too paralyzed to make a financial decision—even if you end up on your own unexpectedly. Knowledge is power, especially when it comes to your money.

Different money experiences you will likely have through your forties and fifties are covered in this book, along with how to make wise choices with that money. Keep in mind that all of the investment examples I've used are just that—they are examples—and are intended to educate you, not give you specific investment advice.

As you read through this book, the advice I'm providing is coming from both my professional experience and personal experience, and I'm passing along this wisdom so you can be happier, more financially secure, and increasingly optimistic about your future. Now, on to you.

Chapter Endnotes:

1. Fidelity Investments. "Money FIT Women Study". 2015. https://www.fidelity.com/bin-public/060_www_fidelity_com/documents/women-fit-money-study.pdf.
2. UBS. "Own your worth. How women can break the cycle of abdication and take control of their wealth". 2018. https://www.ubs.com/content/dam/WealthManagementAmericas/documents/2018-37666-UBS-Own-Your-Worth-report-R32.pdf.
3. McKinsey. "Women as the Next Wave of Growth in Wealth Management Industry". July 29, 2020. https://www.mckinsey.com/industries/financial-services/our-insights/women-as-the-next-wave-of-growth-in-us-wealth-management#.

CHAPTER 1

Step One: What You Need to Know About Money Now

In your twenties and thirties, your financial life may have felt chaotic, confusing, and not well planned out. You were more reactive to your money and money issues instead of being proactive, planning, and controlling your money. It isn't surprising that you would feel out of control when it comes to money in your twenties and thirties, as you were experiencing many big "firsts." First job, first car, first mortgage, first marriage, first baby, and so on. Now, for the most part, your firsts are done.

It's time to really start planning your financial future. You can't afford not to. It's time to get a handle on your money, where you are now, and plan for where you want to go.

If you are married, is your spouse in control of the finances? If so, it's time to change that and educate yourself on the basics. Consider these facts:

- Ninety percent of women will be solely responsible for their finances at some point in their lives following divorce or the death of a spouse.[1]
- Fifty-six percent of married women leave investment decisions up to their spouses.[2]
- Twenty-five percent of affluent women say they are comfortable making investment and savings-related decisions on their own—fifteen percentage points lower than their male counterparts.[3]
- Many married women feel shut out of household wealth discussions; they feel financial advisers reach out to them infrequently or only on matters of day-to-day cash management rather than on bigger investment decisions.[3]

If you are single, you still may not have a great handle on your finances. Women are about 10 percent more likely than men to say they are concerned about outliving their assets in retirement and not having enough savings for retirement.[3]

Let's get started.

Cash, Bank Accounts, and Spending

Determine how many bank accounts you have, the balance in each, and what they are used for. It's usually a good idea to have more than one bank account. The first bank account should be used for paying day-to-day living expenses such as your mortgage, car insurance, utilities, groceries, and other essentials. This is an "in-and-out" account where you don't need to carry a huge balance at the end of each month. A checking account typically doesn't pay a high rate of interest, so it's best to not have all your cash parked there.

An in-and-out checking account also allows you to budget better since you can see whether you are overspending or underspending each month, and how much of what is left could be better directed to a savings account. It's important to have a grasp on how much you are spending each month. I cannot emphasize this enough. Know what your monthly expenses are. No financial adviser can answer your important questions of "Do I have enough?" or "How much longer do I need to work?" or "Do I need to go back to work?" if you can't tell them what your living expenses are.

If you are not the person in your household who pays the bills, take over that responsibility. When a woman gets divorced or becomes a widow, not knowing what the household expenses are or how to pay the bills is a primary reason fear and panic set in. There is no way to know if you have enough money to live independently if you don't know what your living expenses are. I have met so many women over the years, even those in their seventies, who have no idea how to pay a bill. Their father or husband had always taken care of the finances. Knowing what your bills are and how to pay them is critically important for all women, especially married women.

A second bank account should be for savings only. This is often called an emergency fund, which at minimum should equal three to six months of living expenses during your working years. If you don't have a savings account, set one up now. Keep this cash separate from your checking account—and do not withdraw money from this account unless it truly is an emergency, such as losing your job, unexpected medical bills, or a last-minute flight to attend a family funeral. This account should not be used for vacations! As you near retirement, you should have closer to twelve months of living expenses in cash in this savings account. We'll talk more about your rainy day fund throughout the book and why it can remove a substantial amount of stress when life throws you a curveball.

I'm a fan of having a third bank account that can be earmarked for a variety of purposes, such as holiday gifts, vacations, a new car, those shiny diamond earnings you've been eyeing, or any fun expense. You might think of this as an in-and-out account also, but use it to avoid guilt or marital disagreement over the nonessential expenses of your choosing.

Income and Taxes

The ability to earn an income is the single largest asset for most people in their forties and fifties. If you are making $200,000 a year from your job or business, and you multiply that by ten more years of work, that's another $2 million coming your way. Of course, some of that asset will go away, as income tax needs to be paid to the federal and state governments. Income tax rates currently range from 0 percent to 37 percent at the federal level, and when you add in state income taxes and Social Security and Medicare taxes, on the top end, you can be pushing a 50 percent tax rate. Knowing what you have available each year to put toward your financial future starts with knowing what your income and tax situation looks like.

Start by reviewing last year's tax return to see the various ways you and your family make money. Items such as salary, bonus, business income, investment income, and rental property income will be found on a tax return, as well as the amount of tax you pay on that income. Reading a tax return is not easy. The tax return does not provide a simple, clear, and descriptive list of your income and assets, but the return will list (on various pages) the sources of taxable income you have and show most of the sources of taxes you're paying. If you work with an accountant, ask for a meeting to go through your tax return line by line. Take a look at a year-end paystub, which often lists the different types of income earned that year, such as salary, bonus, and stock option income. It also subtracts items you don't pay tax on but still run through a paycheck, such as 401(k) retirement savings contributions, health insurance premiums, and health savings account deposits. The year-end paystub will also show the amount of Social Security and Medicare tax paid during the year, which is not clearly spelled out on a tax return.

I'd encourage you to be the one who gathers all the necessary tax documents each year for preparation of your family's tax return. This will also help ensure you have a firm grip on what income sources you have and the investment accounts or other income-generating assets you own. This is critical information, especially if you are in a shaky marriage or you don't manage the day-to-day finances. Never sign your name on a tax return unless you have taken the time to thoroughly understand each number on that tax return. I've heard stories over the years from women whose spouses were cheating on their tax returns and hiding income or assets—or who were told just to "sign here" while the numbers on the return were kept hidden from them. When you sign your tax return, you are attesting to it being factual, and if it's not, you are committing perjury, which is a crime. Worst case, this can lead to jail time.

Finally, don't assume the amount of tax you are paying is what you *need* to be paying. There are many ways to reduce taxes each year, such as putting more into retirement plans, donating assets more wisely to charity, depositing money into a health savings account, buying tax credits if offered by your state, or deducting certain home office or business expenses. Working with an accountant can be a good move if you are not sure you're taking advantage of all the tax strategies available to you.

Investment Accounts

At this point in your life, you should have already started building savings for retirement in a 401(k), 403(b), SEP IRA, or other retirement savings account. Most people who are working are saving money from each paycheck into their company-sponsored retirement savings account. In your twenties and thirties, you may have only been putting in the minimum amount to get the maximum employer match. For example, if a company contributes up to 3 percent to the 401(k) plan if you contribute at least 6 percent, many people just save that 6 percent. However, now you need to be putting the maximum amount the government allows you to save into your retirement account. In 2021, if you are under age fifty, you can sock away as much as $19,500 into your 401(k) plan. Those age fifty or over can add another $6,500, for a total of $26,000. If you are self-employed, $58,000 or more can be saved into a self-employed retirement account.

Another benefit of ramping up your retirement savings now is it saves taxes. For example, if you are putting $10,000 annually into your before-tax 401(k) account, and are in a 25 percent tax bracket, that saves you $2,500 in taxes each year. If you nearly double your savings to the limit of $19,500, now you are saving $4,875 in tax so it's only "costing" you $14,625 in after-tax dollars to save $19,500 for your retirement. Think of it as the government kicking in some money for your retirement. Putting money into a Roth 401(k) won't save you tax today but withdrawing from this account in retirement can be tax-free under current tax law.

Let's look at an example of long-term savings. Before I begin, some historical context on stock and bond returns is in order. Since 1926 stocks have returned on average 10 percent per year while bonds have returned about 5 percent per year.[4] In the interest of not overinflating expectations about portfolio returns that consist of both stocks and bonds, in my below example, I will assume you earn a hypothetical 6 percent annual return on your investments for illustrative purposes only. Keep in mind past performance is no guarantee of future results.

Example: You are forty years old and have not started saving for retirement. In order to retire at age sixty and have $1,000,000 in your 401(k) account, you'll need to save about $27,000 annually, assuming a hypothetical 6 percent annual investment return. If you wait until age 50 to start saving for retirement, in this example you'd need to save $75,000 annually, which is almost three times as much! The sooner you start saving, the less of your own money you'll need to save due to the benefits of compounded interest. If you've ever heard the phrase "let your money work for you," that's being reflected in my example.

Another great retirement savings account is an IRA or Roth IRA. There are lower savings limits for these accounts: $6,000 in 2021 if you are under age fifty and $7,000 if you are age fifty and above and have earned at least this amount from a job. It doesn't matter if you have a job or your spouse does; only one income is required to put money into each spouse's IRA or Roth IRA each year. There is an income limit that determines whether you are eligible to save money directly into a Roth IRA, but no income limits apply for saving into an IRA. For single individuals whose income is less than $140,000 in 2021, they can contribute the full amount directly to a Roth IRA. This is $208,000 of income for married couples. The benefit of a Roth IRA is withdrawals in retirement are income tax-free as long as you are over age fifty-nine and a half and have had that Roth account open for at least five years.

Let's say you start saving the maximum into your before-tax 401(k) at age forty ($19,500) plus save the maximum each year into your IRA ($6,000). If you do this for twenty years and increase it at age fifty (when the savings limits go up), you'll have accumulated more than $1,100,000 by age sixty, assuming a hypothetical 6 percent annual investment return. Now, most of this $1,100,000 has never been taxed, so when you take money out in retirement, you'll report most of that withdrawal on your income tax return and pay tax. If any of this retirement savings is in a Roth IRA, that leaves more for you to spend and less that goes to the government in tax. Setting a personal goal each year to fully fund retirement accounts, and committing to the goal, will help put you in good financial shape when you are ready to retire.

Another incredibly important goal for many families is saving for their children's college education. I've seen families put the majority of their annual savings into college accounts, neglecting retirement savings. The reason many families justify this is there is a deadline for the college expense—when kids turn age eighteen. There's really no deadline for when you need to retire, so retirement savings takes the back burner. That's not a wise strategy though! I love the phrase "you can finance college, but you can't finance your retirement."

A great way to save money for college is a 529 college savings plan due to the tax benefits. Most states offer a tax deduction for money you deposit into your home state's 529 plan. The money grows tax-deferred inside the 529 so you are not paying taxes on the interest and dividends earned each year. Then, if you take the money out for tuition, books, fees, room and board and other qualified education expenses, all the money comes out tax-free. If there is money left over after your child or children finish college, you can take the balance out for yourself. You'll pay some tax plus a 10 percent tax penalty on the earnings portion, but the tax rate is not much different than you'll pay on retirement withdrawals from your 401(k) or IRA.

Determine how much you can afford to save each year and consider splitting it between retirement and college. Don't totally neglect one savings goal. What happens if you get sick, disabled, or otherwise burned out in your fifties when you thought you had another decade to sock away savings for retirement? We'll talk about this reality more in later chapters.

Finally, most people should have a taxable brokerage account that is invested in stocks and bonds. There is no limit as to what you can save into this account, there are no age restrictions for taking a withdrawal, and the taxes you pay on withdrawals are generally less than you'll pay on before-tax 401(k) or IRA withdrawals. However, you do claim as income on your tax return the interest, dividend, and realized capital gains you earn each year in this brokerage account. A major reason this type of investment account is so important to build is that you can live off these investments if you retire before age fifty-nine and a half. Why is fifty-nine and a half noteworthy? It's the age that you must attain before the 10 percent early withdrawal tax penalty goes away on withdrawals from 401(k), 403(b), SEP IRAs, IRAs, and other retirement savings accounts. Plus, you can keep your tax rate lower in retirement if you can balance the amount of money you withdraw from taxable brokerage accounts and retirement accounts. If the only savings account you have in retirement is a before-tax 401(k), all the withdrawals will be subject to income tax, which means you'll have less to spend on yourself in retirement.

Finally, while it's important to have the right type of savings and investment accounts set up, it's also important to have a solid investment strategy. That is, how much do you have invested in stocks, bonds, real estate, and other long-term investments? When you were in your twenties and thirties it made sense to have most of your investments in stocks due to the long time horizon before you need to spend this money. Now, you are starting to think about retirement and wondering whether you should be more conservative. Or perhaps you are wondering if you have any strategy at all?

One investment strategy that is common, but frightening for me to see, is what I call the "rearview mirror" strategy. It's looking at what investments did well last month, last quarter, or last year, and then putting your money into those. Investing is like planting a garden; different things bloom at different times. Having a diversified mix of investments like US stocks, international stocks, big and small company stocks, real estate, bonds, commodities, cash, etc. makes sense for most people in their forties and fifties. The closer you are to retirement, the more bonds and cash you want. A reasonable asset allocation for people in their forties is about 80 percent stocks or assets that can grow, and 20 percent bonds or other conservative investments. Then, in your early fifties (depending on how close you are to retiring), you can start shifting to a 75 percent/25 percent mix, or a 70 percent/30 percent mix. At retirement, a 50 percent–65

percent stock/growth mix and a 50 percent–35 percent bond/
conservative mix tends to be a reasonable approach for many
people.

Don't forget about rebalancing periodically, which means
realigning your investments to their target percentages, as prices
of investments change over time. For example, if you decide
you want 70 percent in stocks and 30 percent in bonds, and
at the end of the year your 401(k) retirement account is 75
percent stocks and 25 percent bonds, rebalance the account by
moving 5 percent out of stocks (as they went up in value) to 5
percent more in bonds (which didn't go up as much in value).
The opposite can also happen where your 70 percent stock–30
percent bond mix is now 65 percent stocks–35 percent bonds.
In this example, your stocks went down in value that year, so
take 5 percent out of bonds and add it back to stocks. This can
seem counterintuitive, but you are likely buying more stocks
when they are priced low, and then next time you rebalance,
they may have gone up in value, so you take your winnings off
the table and shift them to more conservative bonds.

With investing, you should keep looking forward—not
backward.

Debt

Most people in their forties and fifties have debt, such as a
mortgage or car loan. A mortgage is considered "good debt" as
there is an asset attached to it (your house), which will hopefully
grow in value over time. Other debt is considered "bad debt,"

such as credit cards. At this stage in your life, start thinking more about how to get out of debt rather than eyeing the next bigger home or buying a fancier boat. Just because you are likely making more money now than you did a decade ago, it doesn't mean it's time to ramp up your spending or borrowing to buy bigger things.

Lifestyle creep tends to happen in your forties and fifties, and it's a nasty cycle that's hard to break. If you start experiencing life with the bigger and better things now, like a country club membership, luxury car, more spacious house, vacation home, or flying first class, you will start losing the emotional ability to cut back if times get hard. And you're probably borrowing money to have these nicer lifestyle things, which is adding to the pressure to make more money each year. That can lead to having to work more years and delay retirement, as more of your income is going to pay larger expenses now, and therefore less is available to save for your future.

Rather, in your forties and fifties, start focusing on getting out of debt. How much more do you need to pay each month on your mortgage to eliminate it by the time you want to retire? Do you need a new car every three years—or can you live with yours for seven to ten years? Be sure all student debt is paid off. And if you must have the fanciest, biggest, shiniest new thing, have a plan to pay cash for it versus borrowing money.

If you are drowning in credit card debt in your forties and fifties, you need a major wake-up call. Quit spending money. You are likely in your highest income earning years, so if you can't make ends meet now, you may not be able to earn your way out of that mess. Put a plan in action now to pay off one credit card at a time, starting with the smallest balance credit card. That may sound strange to start with the low-balance card versus the highest-interest rate card. I've found that once people see one credit card completely paid off, it provides the motivation to tackle the next balance until it's down to zero, and so on.

Having available debt can be a good emergency backup plan. For example, keep a home equity line of credit open on your house, but don't pull money from this line of credit unless you get into a major financial jam. Or have a credit card with a much higher credit line than you normally need in case of a major home repair, medical situation, or other emergency where you need access to a lot of cash quickly. The "available debt" sources should just be tucked aside and not considered for day-to-day living; they are more of a sleep-well-at-night safety net move. Hopefully you'll never need to tap into them.

Insurance

Having the right type and amount of insurance throughout your life is necessary to mitigate financial risks. You have lots of insurance needs in your forties and fifties from medical, life, disability, home/auto, liability, and perhaps long-term care insurance. I tend to hear more complaints from people in this stage of life about all the insurance premiums they are paying, than any other stage. However, this is the point in your life where you have assets to protect, but you are still building for your future and need to protect that as well.

Most people get their health, life, and disability insurance through their employer in their forties and fifties. However, especially with life and disability insurance, what your employer offers is often not enough. For example, you are earning $200,000 annually and have $1 million of life insurance through your employer. If something happened to you, that only covers five years of your lost income, but you probably are planning to work at least another ten years. Is there a mortgage to cover, kids' college expenses, or other debts like credit cards or second mortgages that you'd want paid off if you or your loved one dies? Many people think about the mortgage first when determining how much life insurance they need, but replacing the lost paycheck is often the biggest number that needs to go into the equation.

Disability insurance replaces a portion of your income if you are injured or suffer a long-term illness and can't work. Just like life insurance, what your company offers is often not enough to replace your largest asset: your ability to earn an income. Having supplemental life and disability insurance outside your company is often a good move. Plus, if you change jobs and all your life and disability insurance is tied to that prior employer, you may lose it or have to pay an incredibly high premium to take it with you. What if your new dream job does not offer benefits?

On the other hand, with health insurance, what your company offers is usually enough to cover your family. Most employers do offer health insurance, even start-up companies, if they want to attract good talent. Larger employers tend to offer better coverage at better prices than smaller companies, so don't be surprised if you see wide differences in what you're paying for health insurance if you change jobs.

Protecting assets with insurance is done through home, auto, and liability insurance. Having all of these with one company often makes sense to get discounts. Liability insurance is also known as umbrella coverage, and this is needed in case there is a lawsuit against you. For example, you are in a car accident that is your fault. Someone says, "I'm going to sue you for all you're worth." That's where the umbrella policy comes into play as it provides liability protection in the event you are sued. Umbrella coverage comes in increments of $1 million and it is in addition to the basic underlying liability limits found in your homeowners and auto policies. A good rule of thumb is to have umbrella coverage equal to one times your net worth (assets minus debts = net worth). Shop your coverage around every few years and work with an experienced agent to make sure you have the right kind and amount of home/auto/liability coverage.

Buying long-term care insurance used to be a consideration for people when they reached their late fifties or early sixties. This is no longer the case due to the changes this industry has been facing. Now, getting long-term care insurance in place in your forties and fifties is recommended. This type of insurance provides benefits if you are in a nursing home or assisted living facility or need to hire someone to provide home care. These caregiving needs include help feeding, dressing, and bathing you. Most people envision being in their eighties or nineties before they may no longer be able to care for themselves, so they put off purchasing this insurance until much later in life. But if you wait to buy this insurance, it could be too expensive to afford—or you may not qualify due to health issues. The number of companies offering this insurance continues to dwindle, so there's no guarantee you can buy long-term care insurance in the future. Yet these caregiving costs could be the largest financial drain any retiree experiences—and it could financially devastate you. Paying for long-term care insurance is not cheap. You should work with a financial professional in your forties and fifties to determine how to build a budget for all the insurance products you need, how much you need of each, and which to prioritize. As you build more personal assets for retirement, you'll start to find your need for life and disability insurance goes down, and the premiums you were paying for those policies can be shifted to your long-term care budget.

Wills and Trusts

This is an absolute necessity at this point in your life. In the 2018 UBS report, "Own Your Worth," one of their participants lamented about her personal situation: "I don't know how somebody fifty-three years old doesn't have a will and how I let that get past me. So, I am beating myself up now."[2] I have had many people in their forties and fifties come into my office for the first time and shake their heads in embarrassment when

I ask, "Do you have a will?" Unfortunately, it's very common for people to ignore this part of their financial planning.

Every adult needs a will. A will dictates who gets your assets when you pass away and who is responsible for settling your estate. If you have minor children, you name a guardian in your will to care for them if something happens to you. Without a will, you die intestate, and the state you are living in will dictate who receives your money and property.

In addition to a will, every adult needs a financial power of attorney and health care power of attorney. The power of attorney documents control who is in charge of your finances and who can make medical decisions if you are incapacitated and unable to make those decisions yourself.

Many people have trusts set up to have controls over their money once they pass away. If you have substantial assets and life insurance you are leaving to loved ones and want to ensure it's not squandered, a trust can be a good tool in your estate plan. Another reason for a trust is to protect family assets in the event your child gets divorced or is sued. Certain trusts can provide estate tax reduction benefits if you have significant wealth. There are many different types of trusts, and an estate planning attorney can set up an estate plan with the right tools and techniques for your family's needs.

If you don't have an estate plan now, make this a priority and review it every five years or whenever there is a major life change or tax law change.

Chapter Endnotes:

1. Wall Street Journal. "Clients from Venus". 2012. https://www.wsj.com/articles/ SB100014240529702041905045770404020 69714264.

2. UBS. "Own your worth. How women can break the cycle of abdication and take control of their wealth". 2018. https://www.ubs.com/content/dam/WealthManagementAmericas/documents/2018-37666-UBS-Own-Your-Worth-report-R32.pdf.

3. McKinsey. "Women as the Next Wave of Growth in Wealth Management Industry". July 29, 2020. https://www.mckinsey.com/industries/financial-services/our-insights/women-as-the-next-wave-of-growth-in-us-wealth-management#.

4. Vanguard. "Portfolio allocations. Historical index risk/return 1926-2019". https://advisors.vanguard.com/VGApp /iip/advisor/csa/analysisTools/portfolioAnalytics/historicalRiskReturn.

CHAPTER 2

Walking the Tightrope: Balance Living and Saving

After reading chapter 1, you might be feeling overwhelmed. "How can I save for retirement, pay off my mortgage, put my kids through college, have a pile of insurance, get rid of all my debts, and pay a lawyer to update my will? I don't have a money tree in the backyard!" I get it. Don't feel overwhelmed. Here are strategies to balance living today and planning for the future.

First, get your arms around your income, expenses, and taxes as I outlined in the first chapter. Write them down.

Income – Expenses – Taxes = "The Extra"

"The Extra" is the amount you have left to save each year. If "The Extra" is a negative number, you need to go back and figure out how to trim your expenses. I once met a woman who told me her financial plan was to "out earn" her way through her spending problem. She wasn't willing to live differently today to spend less. She was determined to climb the corporate ladder and make more money—and someday catch up to her current lifestyle. That is not a good financial plan for many reasons. First, this individual clearly lacks self-discipline, which is an essential life skill when it comes to managing your finances. If you can't physically stop spending, there's probably something emotional behind that. Why do you feel entitled to live above your means? What is driving your behavior to always want more? Are you putting pressure on yourself to keep up with your social group? Did you lack basic needs growing up and are overcompensating now? Figuring out why you can't stop yourself from overspending should be addressed before you determine your next step to get yourself on track.

If your savings amount is less than 20 percent of your income, I'd encourage you to again trim your expenses. Everyone should try to save at least 20 percent of their before-tax income each year—if not more. Part of this 20 percent can be paying extra on debt such as your mortgage. Try to first save money into accounts that lower your taxes, such as a 401(k) or 403(b) plan through your or your spouse's employer.

Let's look at some examples. Remember:

$$Income - Expenses - Taxes = Savings$$

Example 1: No Savings:

$150,000 − $100,000 − $50,000 = $0 (saving 0 percent of income)

Example 2: Saving $30,000 between a 401(k) plan, health savings account, and an IRA

$150,000 − $80,000 − $40,000 = $30,000 (a better scenario; saving 20 percent of income)

The more money you make over time, the larger the "Income" figure becomes, but don't let that drive increasing the "Expenses" category at the same time. Naturally the more money you make, the more taxes you'll pay, which you have some, but not much, control over. What you can control is your lifestyle and your expenses.

If you get a $50,000 raise, don't change your lifestyle. Save all of the rest of your after-tax raise. Let's add our $50,000 raise into our second example above:

$200,000 − $80,000 − $60,000 = $60,000 (now saving 30 percent of income)

Now you've increased your savings rate to 30 percent of income versus 20 percent before. This will help accelerate your ability to pay for a child's college education and get yourself to retirement.

However, most people don't intentionally have a plan to save "The Extra." They look at what is left over each month and hope they can save it. However, without a plan and carefully monitoring your budget, it's easy for this extra money to get spent. Most people lack the discipline to stick with their savings strategy.

Instead, take the discipline out of the equation, and rework the formula as follows:

Income − Taxes − Savings = Expenses

Make savings more important than spending. Decide how much you want to or need to save each year. Have those savings dollars set up as automatic withdrawals out of your bank account, for the most part. This is how 401(k), 403(b), and health savings accounts through an employer are set up; the amount you elect to save is automatically deducted from your paycheck, and it goes into the applicable savings account each payroll period. So, why not have all your desired monthly savings automatically deducted from your bank account? You can link a bank account to an IRA account and have a set amount transferred into the IRA each month, just as you can with a college savings 529 plan, a regular after-tax brokerage account, your home mortgage, or other debt payments. Once you set up these regular savings, they feel as if they are part of your fixed monthly budget. You get used to not having this cash, and you're less likely to turn the savings amounts off. You will stick with your plan, and you will reap the rewards. Then, as you get your next raise, you'll be able to build a new part of your equation:

New Raise − Taxes − More Savings = Fun Money to Spend

Determine the budget for your new raise or annual bonus before it arrives. Each time you make more money, decide how much you want to save, how much to apply toward debt, and how much you want for "fun money." This may be for home improvement projects, a new car, vacations, gifts to family members, or other uses that aren't required to be saved to meet your financial goals.

CHAPTER 3

Socking it Away in Your Forties and Fifties

Now that you know the basics of a financial plan (chapter 1) and how to build a budget and prioritize savings (chapter 2), the next step is to figure out what "buckets" to put your savings dollars toward. This is a general strategy that will apply to most women in their forties and fifties, single or married, in a professional career or running the household.

First, start with determining when you want to retire. When you were in your twenties and thirties, you may not have given much thought to when you (or you and your spouse/partner) would like to stop working. Now you need to be more serious about planning for this goal. Ultimately, retiring comfortably is a goal all my clients have, and what retiring comfortably looks like is very different from person to person. Would you rather retire early if that means having less money to spend in retirement—or would you rather work longer so that you can fully enjoy the fruits of your labor in retirement with very little financial worry? You're probably thinking, *I want to retire early and have lots of extra money!* Of course! Don't we all?

Start to pinpoint a date in the future that could reasonably work with your lifestyle. If you have children, maybe the retirement date is when the last child graduates from college, or perhaps it's enjoying a more measured work-life balance for a few years after the last child graduates. People often line up their retirement date with the date their home mortgage is set to be paid off. I've heard others say, "There is no way I'm working into my seventies like my parents did." As you progress through your forties and fifties, unfortunately you are going to be faced with the sad reality of seeing some of your friends or peers pass away prematurely. This will get you thinking harder about retiring early since tomorrow is not promised to anyone—and you want to be able to enjoy as many of the good retired years as you can.

Once you've determined your retirement date, calculate the amount of money it's going to take to pay your bills in retirement. Divide this between fixed expenses and variable expenses. While I cover this in detail in my first book, generally things like utilities, property taxes, and insurance are fixed expenses. Variable expenses are vacations, gifts, new cars, etc. At this point in time, it may be wise to hire a financial professional to run the retirement calculations. One thing is for certain with retirement calculations—the most important input into the equation is someone's desired living expenses in retirement. The higher this number, the more money you need saved for retirement or the longer you need to work to build up enough savings. The retirement living expense number will certainly evolve and be easier to pinpoint the closer you are to retirement. For now, take a reasonable estimate of what you are spending, subtract the expenses that will disappear, like higher family grocery bills or the mortgage payment, and increase the discretionary spending assumption (since every day in retirement will feel like a Saturday, which is when many working adults spend most of their discretionary money).

A rough rule of thumb is to take your after-tax annual living expense number, add in taxes, and divide that sum by 4 percent. This "4 percent rule" is a fairly conservative calculation assuming someone lives thirty years in retirement. The 4 percent calculation will tell you how much money you need saved before you retire. For example, if you need to pay yourself a salary of $100,000 annually in retirement, you need an investment portfolio of $2,500,000 to support that for a thirty-year retirement. (Factor in pension and Social Security income if you want to count on those in your retirement or run the calculation with and without pension and Social Security income).

For example, when you retire, you want to spend $150,000 annually. Adding in taxes, let's say you need to pay myself a salary of $200,000 per year. You will plan on $40,000 annually from Social Security. That means you need to withdraw $160,000 annually from your investment portfolio. $160,000 / 4 percent = $4,000,000 which is your retirement savings number.

Once you've nailed down the amount you need saved for retirement, if you have children and plan to pay for their college, pull together that calculation. These expenses are hard to predict the further you are from kids going off to college, but it's best to start with some assumptions. Do you want to fund four years of public college or private university costs? In-state or out-of-state tuition? I often see parents use the assumption of their alma mater as a starting point for calculating what college may cost for their family. Then, you can back into what you need to save each year (again a good time to enlist a financial professional if you want help in putting the calculation together).

Next, what other short-term or long-term goals do you have? Putting a pool in the backyard? Helping a family member financially? Donating more to charity? Whatever your individual goals may be, write them down on a timeline and attach a dollar figure to what they'll cost.

Also factor in paying off debt. How much do you have and how soon is reasonable to eliminate the debt? If it's your mortgage, plan to get this paid off by the time you retire.

Here is a sample financial goal timeline:

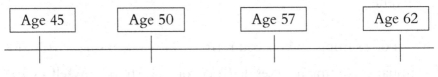

| Age 45 | Age 50 | Age 57 | Age 62 |

Pool in Backyard   College Funded   Mortgage Paid Off   Retire

With this timeline in place, you can start prioritizing what "buckets" your monthly or annual savings dollars go toward. A hint! Don't put every dollar of savings toward the first goal on your timeline! Spread your savings out so you are putting money toward all your future goals and do not sacrifice retirement savings just because it's the furthest out on your timeline.

For any goals within two to five years, save that money in cash or CDs. Don't try to make a quick dollar by investing it in the stock market since you don't want a down market to hit at the same time you're needing the cash to pay for the pool, in my above example.

As mentioned in chapter 1, with college savings, 529 plans are typically the way to go. Each state offers them, and most states offer a tax incentive for its residents to open the 529 plan in their home state. Encourage family members to contribute to the 529 plan for your child or children in lieu of bigger holiday or birthday gifts. These plans have age-based investment strategies that are an easy way for investors to be in a reasonable investment mix without having to worry about changing it over time. With the age-based investment strategies, the younger your child, the more stocks are in the account. As your child gets older, stocks shift to bonds so that the account is conservative by the time he or she goes to college. You just sit back and focus on saving money in the 529 plan account.

Paying off your mortgage early requires making some extra payments each year. The easiest approach is to increase the amount you pay monthly, so extra is going to pay down principal each month. Increase the extra you pay in principal each year, especially as you get raises.

For retirement savings, many types of accounts are available. Start with those your employer offers, such as a 401(k) or 403(b) plan, SEP IRA, Simple IRA, or deferred compensation account, especially if the employer makes a matching contribution. Strive to put the maximum amount allowed into your company-sponsored retirement accounts each year. Most of this savings will be deducted automatically from your paycheck, so it's an easy way to save and doesn't take much self-discipline to make it happen.

As covered in chapter 1, establish additional retirement savings accounts such as IRAs, Roth IRAs, and taxable brokerage accounts. Make it a goal to sock money away in these accounts for retirement in addition to what you are saving inside employer-sponsored retirement accounts. While there are limits as to what you can save into an IRA or Roth IRA each year, and that limit tends to increase every few years, there is no limit on what you can save in a taxable brokerage account. While investing money in a taxable brokerage account won't save you tax now, you'll pay less tax on this type of money when you withdraw it in retirement.

Finally, health savings accounts (HSAs) are a tremendous retirement savings vehicle. An HSA should be viewed as a retirement savings account and not as a current-day medical spending account. The HSA has a "triple tax play" whereby you save tax on the money you deposit each year (up to annual limits), there is no tax on the interest the money earns while inside the account, and when you withdraw money to pay for qualified medical expenses, the money comes out tax-free. Let's look at an example:

$10,000 medical bill in retirement:

Option 1) Take $15,000 out of my 401(k), pay the tax, and come out with $10,000.

Option 2) Take $10,000 out of my HSA as it's tax-free!

I've found the best way to manage all of your savings goals is to set a disciplined strategy, so you know what "buckets" money will go into, and at what percent, every time you have extra money to save. Look at this sample strategy:

Funding a Savings Strategy

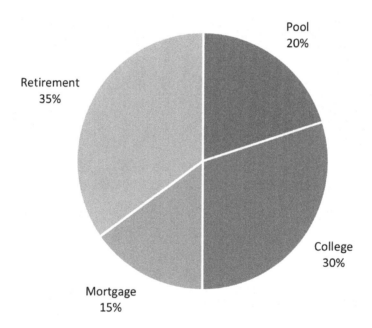

As you accomplish each of these goals, you can adjust your savings percentages to start tackling the next goals. Don't start saving less; instead, reposition which "buckets" you are saving money into going forward. It will feel great to have a plan in place—and you're more likely to see the results faster!

CHAPTER 4

Climbing the Ladder at Work

If you are a career girl, this phase of life is where you hit your stride. You figure out what work-related activities energize you—and hopefully find a group of people you love working with. Many career-oriented women find fulfillment and satisfaction from their work that they don't get in other parts of their life. According to a 2019 study from the Center for Creative Leadership, what women want from their work is to find their calling, to have flexibility in when, where, and how they work, and to have real leadership opportunities. Women want to make a difference on their terms.[1] If you've got all of these going for you, "company rock star" may be the correct nickname for you!

It wasn't easy getting to where you are now. While the future looks bright, you no doubt won't forget how you got to where you are. Did someone look behind, grab your hand,

and pull you forward? Did you have to claw and scrape your way to the next rung of the ladder? And have you been smart about making the most of each raise, bonus, stock award, and company perk? As you reflect on where you've been and where you are now, the people and the money involved both matter tremendously—and hopefully you'll keep that perspective as you propel forward in your personal and financial life.

The career girls in my professional and personal circle have very similar traits. We really enjoy the type of work we do, we're not hopping around much searching for the next best thing, and we've found a way to balance work and home life in a messy but productive way. We all agree we're not perfect at any one of our life's priorities, and there's never enough time. But we also can't imagine giving up what we've worked so hard for—even as the tears roll down our faces when we can't be as present for our children. There's always guilt that we're not doing enough, so we do more, only to have more guilt. But we're still proud of who we are, what we contribute to this world and our families, and how we lead. None of the women in my circles want to keep working forever, and we do want to know our hard work is paying off now *and* in the future.

That's why financial planning is so important. According to a 2018 article by Business Insider, women hit their peak earnings at age forty. (For men, it's age forty-nine). On average, women who become 401(k) millionaires reach that milestone at age 58.5, earning an average salary of just over $287,000.[2] Your forties and fifties are the key years to sock away money and grow your nest egg so you can enjoy the fruits of your labor in retirement.

Make sure you are saving your raises and not spending them. Keeping up with the Joneses is such an unfortunate reality when people start climbing the corporate ladder; they feel like it's their right or an expectation to live a bigger lifestyle. Don't get sucked into this trap.

All working women climbing the ladder should be striving to put the maximum amount of money into their 401(k) plans, IRAs, and other available retirement savings plans. This also includes nonqualified or supplemental savings plans for high-income earners such as deferred compensation accounts. The more you can push yourself to save now, the greater the lifelong rewards will be. Plus, you can save a boatload of taxes by socking away money in before-tax retirement accounts. The higher you climb at work, the more financial rewards and benefit programs will be available to you. Take advantage of them.

While big money rolling in can feel great, there's no guarantee it will last. You could lose your job, get sick, have a family member get sick that you need to care for, or encounter another major twist that causes a sudden exit from the workforce. Now is the time to set yourself up for maximum lifetime flexibility.

Seek out professional advice if you haven't already done so and have a plan for what to do with your income. One of the most common regrets I hear from new clients in their forties, fifties, and sixties is not getting their financial affairs in order and saving earlier in life. They say, "I wish I had done this years ago." Learn from others' regrets and plow ahead now.

Getting Involved with Charity

Another trait many professional women in their forties and fifties have in common is the desire to give back. As I mentioned above, many of us remember the people who reached behind them and pulled us forward, and we are thankful for the financial comforts we have earned. We understand not all people are as fortunate, and it's our duty to give some of our time, talent, and treasure to support causes we care about. Professional women often ask me how I find the time to volunteer, serve, and lead in the nonprofit world. They share with me their desire to get involved with charity, but they don't know where to start. Giving of your time and leading in the nonprofit world is in essence a business activity; it builds your personal brand. If you look at leaders of many organizations, they serve in the nonprofit world. Bill Gates is one of the most iconic business leaders who grew a successful Fortune 500 company (Microsoft) *and* established a massive nonprofit (Bill and Melinda Gates Foundation). He left corporate America to lead in the philanthropic world, and he now focuses his energies on poverty, inequality, infectious diseases, and many other important causes. Another great example is Arthur Blank, cofounder of The Home Depot, and his Arthur M. Blank Foundation. His nonprofit supports a wide variety of community-development programs, underserved youth, health care initiatives, the arts, environmental issues, and many more. Oprah Winfrey's foundation has a specific focus on youth education and has been around since 1993. Female American novelist Mackenzie Scott (formerly Bezos) is sixth on

Forbes' most generous billionaires list as of 2020, and has signed a pledge to give at least half of her wealth to charity.

You don't need to be as iconic as these influencers to make a huge impact. Don't look at volunteering as trying to fit something else into your busy schedule; instead, consider it an investment in yourself. Serving others is extremely gratifying. And if you are a parent, wow, what a message you are sending to your children.

Where do you start? Figure out the causes that motivate you—is it homelessness, animals, early childhood education, cancer, or disabilities? Start asking friends or colleagues if they know of any charitable organizations in those areas and who they can connect you with. Begin with one volunteer project, take a tour of the facility, participate in a fundraiser, join a committee, and then if you feel compelled, join the board of directors. Expect to make a financial gift each year if you are supporting a charitable organization, especially if you serve on the board of directors. Don't get involved because you want to make more contacts or try to sell your product or service to other people there. People will see right through you, and your brand will be damaged. Those connections will come naturally because you share a passion for the same cause. If you allocate your time to support charitable causes, it's likely to help spring you up a few more rungs of the ladder in your professional life.

Mentorship

Finally, find a mentor and be a mentor. I believe learning is a lifelong process. Even though you may be at the top of your game, there are still new professional and personal life experiences coming your way, which other successful women have already gone through. Maybe it's navigating the next step up the ladder at work, figuring out how to care for elderly parents while maintaining your job, or finding your replacement so you can feel good about retiring and not leaving your company in the lurch. Take all that you've learned and help someone behind you—male or female. It's important to teach and nurture your children—and younger coworkers. I've been amazed over the years how a small gesture on my part can have a lasting impact on younger colleagues. They say, "Remember when you told me to fire a rude client as a good one will come along? You were right." Or "You said don't spend too much time at the office and miss your son's baseball game. Well, he hit his first home run last night!" And "My wife thanks you for being so understanding when I need to leave for a sick child. She just got a big promotion." Being a mother has given me an extra layer of grace to extend to my younger coworkers, and whether you are a parent or not, remember the struggles you had coming up through the ranks. Be gracious, be patient, and be aware of who needs your help. You never know when they will surpass your career pinnacle and go on to achieve extraordinary things.

Chapter Endnotes:

1. Center for Creative Leadership. "Women in the Workplace. Why Women Make Great Leaders & How to Retain Them". 2019. https://www.ccl.org/articles/leading-effectively-articles/7-reasons-want-women-workplace/.

2. Business Insider. "Here are the ages you financially peak at everything throughout life – from salary to net worth". 2018. https://www.businessinsider.com/when-you-earn-the-most-owe-the-most-and-accrue-the-most-wealth-2017-12.

CHAPTER 5

Giving Up Your Career

If you are a career girl, at some point in your life, you may have considered jumping out of career mode. In your early thirties, raising children may have been your motivation to consider leaving the workforce. Now, perhaps your spouse or partner has plowed ahead with their career—or your job is not fulfilling—and it feels like a good time to put the brakes on your career. Or maybe your schedule is extremely hectic, and you find yourself asking, "How long can I keep going at this pace?" It's tough to find the right balance for your family. I know—I'm living through it.

I've seen many couples make the "one career or two" decision when they have their first child, but a handful are pivoting later in their careers, even those without the demands of raising children. Part of this pivot, I believe, is attributable to the fast-paced world we live in. There's only so long you can run hard on the hamster wheel of life before burning out or experiencing health issues. The other reason is caregiving for children, parents, and sometimes a spouse whose health is failing early in life.

I'll begin helping you think through this major decision of whether to give up your career now with an excerpt from my first book—*Girl Talk, Money Talk. The Smart Girl's Guide to Money After College*—and then we'll move into other considerations for women in their forties and fifties later in this chapter.

> I'm forty-one years old at the time I'm writing this book, and I struggle with whether I made the right decision to be a working mom every single day of my life! In truth, while there is a critical time in your life to make this decision—it's often right before or during your maternity leave with your first child—it's a decision most women struggle with for the rest of their lives. Yes, I said rest of their lives!
>
> Early on, the struggle will range from being away from your baby to give a sales presentation, seeing your child cry for your nanny or husband and not for you, or experiencing that disappointment on your child's face when you are the only mom who missed their third-grade musical performance. Then, as the years pass, your child might not come to you with questions or problems because they don't know what time you'll be home from work

that night or what day you'll be back from your business trip. They may start spending more time with their friends and not want to be around their parents anymore. You might start regretting all those hours you weren't home to watch them grow up and hug them.

Then, when you are older and retired and possibly have grandchildren, there will certainly be times when you reflect back and think about what you could have done better—or differently—and whether you had the impact on the world you wanted to have. Did you impact the people you love positively? Did you spend the right amount of time with your spouse, your kids, and your job? This balance is what "having it all means" to so many women. It's having a happy family life and a fabulous career.

You will likely change your mind a multitude of times about career versus family life for the next eighteen years—or more—when you have children living in your home. Women tend to want it all and think they can have it all. There have been many books written about the ability to have it all. As each day passes, you may totally change your perception of whether you have it all or what you can do differently to have it all. Balancing family and work life is a major challenge. You are trying to balance two incredibly fulfilling and personally defining elements of life.

For a career-oriented young woman, the decision to be a working mom or a stay-at-home mom may be the single largest personal decision you'll ever make. It has massive impacts on so many areas of your own life—personal identity, personal happiness, life satisfaction, self-esteem, and a sense of belonging. The emotional tug-of-war between balancing work life and family life pulls at any woman's heart if she needs to be away from her children to earn a paycheck.

If you haven't processed this give-up-my-career-or-not decision yet, now that you are in your forties and fifties, there are even more personal dimensions and family dynamics to add to the thought process.

According to a 2019 article in *Forbes*, "Why Women Quit", the author points out that working women are:[1]

- twice as likely as their male counterparts to run the household
- three times more likely to manage their children's schedules
- eight times more likely to require time off to care for a sick child
- three times as likely to volunteer for school or community activities

Working women work a "third shift" while continuing to have high expectations of performance at their paying jobs. The bottom line is that working women are exhausted!

Running on this hamster wheel of life is exhausting and can lead to daydreaming about an easier way of life—or how soon you can retire. The stress in a marriage can be intense, and if you find running two careers is wearing you both down, it could be time to reassess. Your children will pick up on the marital stress, and they don't want to see their parents' relationship collapse, especially at this point in their lives.

Financial considerations are paramount to making the important go-or-no-go career decision. You are likely in the height of your expense needs—mortgage, groceries, health insurance, family vacations, private school tuition, and other ancillary items. Plus, you see the big-ticket expenses coming like college education(s). "How can we afford to give up one paycheck and not have to drastically change our lifestyle today?" "What will this do to our children?" "Will we ever be able to retire?" These are legitimate questions and money often dictates how couples make the decision to give up someone's career or not. This is the time in your life where you should be thinking about your long-term goals for retirement. At what age do you want this to happen? How big do you want your retirement lifestyle to be? If you sacrifice income and savings now, are you OK working longer and delaying retirement? A financial plan can give you perspective on all of these questions—and right now could be a great time to have some numbers run.

We've talked about the importance of avoiding lifestyle creep as you make more money, and this career decision is much harder if you are living a big lifestyle. Does it take 100 percent of both salaries to run the house? There simply may not be an option to give up a paycheck, financially, at least in the near term. More stress and resentment can flare up if money is putting demands on one or both careers to keep running hot. For married couples, it takes both partners to agree how and when to reduce expenses in order to give up one paycheck or allow one partner to make less money. Which partner is giving up their income versus who is giving up more on the living expense side? For example, if one spouse likes to golf, but that's deemed one area to cut back so that the other spouse can work fewer hours and make less, will the first spouse lay a guilt trip on the other spouse? Each spouse needs to feel they are giving up a similar amount on the expense side and be OK with who is able to have a less stressful, slower-paced, lower-income lifestyle.

Additionally, if you are exhausted at this point in your life and think you'd like a break from your career—but will go back one day—consider the statistics on lost wages and challenges of reentering the workforce:

- According to the *Center for American Progress,* if a woman age 40 making $100,000 annually takes five years off from work, and then returns, it will cost her $668,000 when you factor in the impact of lost wage growth too.[2]
- A 2015 study by the National Bureau of Economic Research found "robust evidence of age discrimination

against older women," especially those nearing retirement age.[3]

- The "motherhood penalty"—a pay gap that has barely budged in thirty years—is costing women $16,000 a year in lost wages, according to a 2018 analysis of US Census data by the National Women's Law Center, a nonprofit advocacy organization. Mothers in the United States get paid seventy-one cents for every dollar their male counterparts make.[4]

- According to a 2018 *Harvard Business Review* study, stay-at-home moms are half as likely to land a job interview compared to moms who had been laid off.[5]

The longer you are out of the workforce, the greater the impact on your future financial well-being. Each year you are not adding to retirement savings can equal multiple more years that you need to work before you can afford to retire. For example, if you are saving $25,000 annually toward your retirement, assuming a moderate 6 percent rate of investment return, after five years, that equates to $140,000 in retirement savings. If you work straight through for ten years at this savings pace, that equates to $329,000—well more than double where you were five years ago. During this time, the value of compounded interest—or investing your money wisely—is $80,000. That is a real cost of leaving the workforce.

If you leave the workforce and stop saving into your retirement account during that time, every year of borrowed time will extend the age you can retire. Let's say I'm burned out at forty-five and plan to take five years off. If I start back at fifty, I'll probably need to work until age sixty-two to have the same amount of retirement savings as I would have had if I had plowed through and worked from forty-five to fifty-three and retired at age fifty-three. The later the age you jump off the hamster wheel, even temporarily, the harder it will be to jump back into the game, especially full-time. There is going to be an earnings gap as your skills and knowledge haven't kept pace with someone living and breathing all the work changes—even for a gap lasting one or two years. You likely won't reenter at the same pay as before or with equally lucrative benefits. There could be bias barriers to overcome from men and women who have been juggling work and life straight through. Then again, perhaps you won't care to have such a high-strung career going forward and are looking for something with a slower pace—without advancement possibilities or a ladder to climb. You won't know how you'll change during your gap years or what you'll want coming out of the gap years—or if you'll even want to reenter the workforce. From a financial standpoint, it's a wise move to run various scenarios, such as going back to work full-time, part-time, or not at all before you decide to leave the workforce.

This is a very difficult decision for any woman who has been career focused up to this point in her life. Do your research, talk with friends or mentors who have taken the leap, connect with an executive or career coach, and keep the lines of communication very open between you and your spouse or partner. Once you've made the decision, have a plan to revisit it every six months to make sure it's still working for you and your family.

Chapter Endnotes:

1. Forbes. "Why Women Quit". August 21, 2019. https://www.forbes.com/sites/lizelting/2019/08/21/why-women-quit/?sh=1a30835d16fa.
2. Center for American Progress. "The Hidden Cost of the Failing Child Care System". https://interactives.americanprogress.org/childcarecosts/.
3. Bloomberg Economics. "Women Face Age Discrimination Earlier and More Often Than Men". October 27, 2015. https://www.bloomberg.com/news/articles/2015-10-27/women-face-age-discrimination-earlier-and-more-often-than-men.
4. National Women's Law Center. "Mothers Lose $16,000 Annually to the Wage Gap". May 23, 2018. https://nwlc.org/press-releases/mothers-lose-16000-annually-to-the-wage-gap-nwlc-analysis-shows/.
5. Harvard Business Review. "Stay-at-Home Moms are Half as Likely to Get a Job Interview as Moms Who Got Laid Off". February 22, 2018. https://hbr.org/2018/02/stay-at-home-moms-are-half-as-likely-to-get-a-job-interview-as-moms-who-got-laid-off.

CHAPTER 6

Boom. Planning for the Financial Unexpected

You can have the best financial plan with the best intentions of following it every single year, but inevitably, life will throw you a curveball. And these curveballs have varying price tags that come along with them.

Some of the smaller curveballs are things like a leaky faucet that requires a plumber to fix or a check engine light that requires maintenance by a mechanic. Hopefully, these minor headaches can be paid for with regular monthly cash flow—and you don't need to dip into your emergency savings to cover them. But if you do, but sure to quickly replenish the amount of cash you took out of savings to pay for the small, unexpected expenses.

Then there's the big, unexpected curveballs. These life-changing curveballs can be personal, emotional, or financial. Big and stressful curveballs can include a job loss, an economic downturn, a hurricane that rips the roof off your house, a major car accident that's your fault, or an unfortunate medical diagnosis. As hard as it will be to plow forward, it's extraordinarily easier if you have financial resources in your back pocket. These inevitable bumps in the road further argue why you never want to deplete your emergency cash reserves or let them dip below a base level that gives you comfort. If you've planned in advance, you can remove one unnecessary layer of stress—the financial stress—when navigating these challenges.

Imagine hearing you just lost your job. Many different schools of thought can run through your mind, and they'll change based on how well you've planned your finances up to this point. "How am I going to pay my mortgage or the kids' private school tuition?" Alternatively, picture a more peaceful and positive approach: "Well, let's use this time to take a family vacation where I don't need to be tied to my phone!" or "Maybe now is the time for me to take a few months and explore the real estate career I've been interested in." Even better, if you have saved well and prepared for the unexpected, you may find retiring a few years earlier than expected is a viable option. When one door closes, another one opens. Being financially secure at any stage in your life can help you more confidently walk through the next door.

The time to be focused on planning for the financially unexpected is when times feel good and easy. Perhaps your family business is steady and growing at a nice pace or your company's stock price keeps going up and up—and your bonuses do too. Don't rest on your laurels; instead, count your blessings and start planning for the rainy day. Sock money away in savings when money is freely flowing toward you.

Recessions and the Stock Market

Over the last 150 years, on average a recession happens about every five years.[1] A recession is when the economy slows down and has negative growth. On average a recession lasts about 1.5 years.[2] The stock market typically slows down and can have negative returns during a recession. When stocks decline by 20 percent or more, the stock market enters a "bear market." During a bear market, stock prices on average fall by 36 percent.[3] Bear markets are a normal part of the investing cycle. This is extremely important to understand before you start investing or take control of an existing investment portfolio. While nobody enjoys seeing the value of their investments go down temporarily, it will happen again and again. In fact, the average person will experience fourteen bear markets during their fifty-year investing lifetime.[4]

When stock prices climb by 20 percent or more from their low point, you'll hear the phrase "bull market" to describe that part of the cycle. On average, stock prices gain 112 percent during the average bull market.[3] Over the past ninety-one years, stocks have had positive returns 77 percent of the time.[3] As you can see, historically, the good times have far exceeded the bad times when it comes to investing.[5]

There's no red flag that gets raised alerting you to when economic growth will slow and the recession will start. Nor can anyone accurately and consistently predict when the stock market will decline, unemployment rates will rise, a health pandemic will unexpectedly throw the world into chaos, or consumer confidence will drop and people will have less money to spend, further slowing the economy. Since these inevitable slowdowns will occur, get your financial house in order before they happen and make sure you have enough cash in the bank to weather through.

A Timely Example: COVID-19

As I write this book, the world has been experiencing one of those big, unsettling, unexpected financial changes as a result of COVID-19. In what felt like a matter of a few weeks in 2020, in the US, we went from the stock market reaching an all-time high in February to a 30 percent drop in March. Then, almost ten million people filed for unemployment in a two-week period, numbers this country hadn't seen since the Great Depression more than ninety years ago. Restaurants and boutique shops rapidly closed their doors, dentists could not serve patients, large department stores were on the brink of collapse, gas prices plummeted, and almost every working adult was relegated to working from home. While financial professionals had been saying for years that a recession was overdue, it was hard for many people to comprehend it coming anytime soon because life had been feeling really good and stable for so many years leading up to 2020. Unemployment rates were extremely low, it had been more than eleven years since we experienced the last bear market, and the housing market had been booming. Nobody knew the coronavirus would be the precipice that would turn our world upside down and trigger the next economic slowdown—and nobody knew how long the slowdown would continue or whether it will have long-term financial impacts.

During my twenty-year career in the financial services profession, I've listened to clients, over and over, comment about how they experienced the dot-com bust of the late 1990s and early 2000s and what they did during the 2008-2009 Great Recession. COVID-19 will be another time that people will remember for its financial impact and how they reacted. These emotionally and financially challenging times in history are hard to totally forget, especially if you did not fare well during them. Some people learn lessons from making mistakes, others drag fear around with them and have a pessimistic view of the future, and others brag about predicting the bust and getting ahead of everyone else.

The ways you are likely to respond in the future depend on how severely an economic downturn impacts you—and whether you coast through them. I recall one person telling me how smart he was when he "sold out" of his stocks in 2007 right before the financial world started to unravel in 2008. But he also sat on that cash for too many years and missed the run-up in stock prices in 2009. By the time he "got back in" to the stock market with his retirement savings, stock prices had shot up—and he was paying more for stocks than the prices he sold them at in 2007. That's called buying high and selling low, which is a guaranteed way to lose money.

When it comes to predicting stock market moves, if you guess correctly once, it's nearly impossible to guess correctly twice. And if you let your emotions drive your financial decisions, you're likely to make a blunder. Instead, before you jump to any conclusions when life throws you a big curveball, take several days or weeks to contemplate whether you should change anything with your money, make a list of the pros and cons, talk with a professional or trusted friend/family member, and take a deep breath. If you've planned well for a rainy day, chances are very low that anything should change with your financial plan. You may need to tap into your emergency fund savings, but then again, that's why you have it.

If you haven't planned in advance and don't have enough cash in the bank to ride out the storm, there are a few strategies to jump on. First, make a list of your bottom-line fixed monthly expenses such as your mortgage, utility bills, debt payments, and groceries. Understand the bare-bones minimum you need to get by and look at what liquid financial resources you could tap, if not cash in the bank. While not ideal, is there a 401(k) plan you could take a loan against or early withdrawal from? Do you have children's 529 plan college accounts that otherwise don't need to be touched for several more years or have money left over in them? Do you have equity in your home you could tap into through a home equity line of credit? Perhaps you have an old life insurance policy that has cash value you can borrow against. If you are fortunate enough to have family members who are financially stable, a family loan with an agreed upon payback schedule is an option. Money and family can get very sticky, so make sure you've communicated up-front about the expectation for interest being paid, the time frame for paying this money back, and what happens if your "storm" lasts longer than expected and you can't pay it back on time. You don't want family holidays to be awkward with this debt burden hanging over you that you're trying to avoid discussing.

Next, a phone call to your mortgage or other debt companies may be in order to attempt working out a reduced or modified monthly payment plan. Depending upon the severity of the financial slowdown in the world, you may find these debt companies already have programs in place to help temporarily. Banks may have loan programs you can apply for as well. Try to keep making your basic monthly payments so your credit doesn't get destroyed and impact you for several years.

It can be extremely stressful to navigate life's uncertainties, but if you can build a financial cushion in advance and set money aside, you are less likely to panic and make big money mistakes. You're also more likely to have a glass-half-full approach to your future and easily leave those past bumpy moments behind.

Chapter Endnotes:

1. Federal Reserve Bank of New York. "Forecasting the Frequency of Recessions". 2006.
2. Forbes. "Recession is Overdue by 4.5 Years, Here's How to Prepare". October 23, 2018. https://www.forbes.com/sites/

cameronkeng/2018/10/23/recession-is-overdue-by-4-5-years-heres-how-to-prepare/?sh=4c3053240d8a.

3. Hartford Funds. "10 Things You Should Know About Bear Markets". 2020. https://www.hartfordfunds.com/practice-management/client-conversations/bear-markets.html.

4. Economist. "How Long Will the Expansion Last". August 16, 2014. https://www.economist.com/united-states/2014/08/16/how-long-will-the-expansion-last.

5. Past performance is not a guarantee of future investment returns.

CHAPTER 7

Three Big Money Mistakes To Avoid

While everyone's personal circumstances are different, there are three major money mistakes I've commonly seen people in their forties and fifties make. These mistakes can totally derail a person's financial future. If you can at least have an awareness of what these are, you are more likely to avoid heading toward them before it's too late.

Money Mistake 1: Owning Too Much House

Owning too much house comes in two varieties. The first is buying a house that's too big or too expensive for your financial situation. I often see people who start making more money in their thirties and forties upgrade to larger and more expensive homes, feeling like they can afford a grander lifestyle. What they are overlooking is the long-term negative impact this can have on their financial future, their ability to retire, their flexibility to weather financial storms, and the emotional toll it will take on their family if they are forced to downsize sooner than they'd want.

For most families, the home is one of the largest fixed monthly expenses in their budget. The mortgage is a primary expense, but you also need to add in property taxes and homeowners insurance. Plus, as all homeowners know, there is an ongoing list of repairs and maintenance costs such as replacing the roof, a leaky faucet, painting needs, new carpet, or staining hardwood floors. Then there are the larger and painful expenses like a hot water heater that leaks and floods the basement, resulting in thousands of dollars of repairs and/ or insurance headaches. While all these expenses are somewhat expected as homeowners, the timing is often unexpected. It's easy to find yourself with extra cash on hand to save for your future and then needing to tap into it to pay for home repairs. A liquid asset (cash) turns into an illiquid asset (house). A home really is an illiquid asset. You can't buy groceries with the equity in your home unless you pull out the equity and saddle yourself with long-term debt.

A good rule of thumb is to have your real estate portfolio equal to less than 30 percent of your total assets. A long-term goal of any homeowner should be to pay off their mortgage before they retire to minimize their monthly fixed expenses. This gives people more freedom and financial flexibility in retirement to spend their money on leisure activities, travel, and medical needs. When economic times sour in retirement, the lower your fixed monthly expenses, the greater the odds that you can reduce your living expenses until the stock market and your investment portfolio recovers.

I once had a client who owned a $500,000 home in a comfortable, suburban area just outside the major city limits. He had a good job, four children, and was the sole income earner for the family. He grew up poor and didn't have a stable family life, which I believe contributed to the big mistake he was about to make. He found his career taking off and decided to upgrade the family home with his newfound income. This is where his financial future started to unravel. As the architect's plans were being drawn, the couple continued to make modifications to add more "bells and whistles." The property they purchased to build their new home on was located in a posh section inside the city. The ultimate price tag of their masterpiece was six times the price tag of the home they had just moved out of. This new home cost $3 million. They borrowed nearly every penny from the bank to build their McMansion. Suddenly, the housing market turned south, and home values stayed low for several years in that expensive area. His income, while still incredibly high, didn't grow at the rate he had hoped. Within one year of building this extravagant home, their balance sheet was negative—and it took them several years to get the mortgage balance down to a level where they had positive equity in their home. Can you imagine the stress this caused the sole breadwinner to have to work harder and harder—fearing he may lose his job one day and what that would do to his family? They could not realistically cut back their lifestyle because their monthly cash flow needs were nearly all fixed expenses. Their monthly mortgage payment was more than some people make in an entire year in this country. And he was too embarrassed to talk about the mistake he made, which caused him a lot of anxiety and health issues.

While this example is more extreme, it points to the fact that emotions can outweigh logic when it comes to what you want your home to be for your family, which can lead to costly financial mistakes.

Money Mistake 2: Owning Too Many Houses

I have a strong opinion about whether someone should own more than one home—and the answer almost always is No! As I mentioned above, real estate brings along higher fixed monthly expenses, which curtails anyone's financial flexibility, especially when life throws you a curveball. Consider having two sets of insurance and property taxes, two dishwashers that can break, two houses that need painting, new roofs, windows, driveways paved, landscaping work, and the list goes on.

I do understand the attraction to owning a second home. This residence is usually located in one's "happy place," like the beach or mountains, and is an escape from reality. When you go on vacation you can relax, and hopefully turn off technology to rejoice in nature. You're surrounded by things you love or love doing. Who doesn't want more of that in their lives?

Over the years I've had clients essentially try to sell me on why it makes sense for them to buy a second home. The common sales pitches are:

- It's a great investment! We can rent it out when we're not using it to cover our mortgage, so it's essentially free!
- We'll hold family reunions here, and the house will be a multigenerational retreat. The kids and grandkids will all come for Thanksgiving each year and a week or two in the summer.
- This house can be left to our kids in our will—so we're also passing down memories!
- It's on sale! The owner just dropped the price so we are getting it cheap!
- Isn't it better to buy it now since prices will probably go up in the future? You know, we can get part of our retirement plan in place now (even though we can't use it much now given our hectic schedules).

For each of these arguments, I have a counterargument—or let's call it an "alternative perspective."

Regarding a second home being a great investment, let's make sure we're looking at all the costs involved. Will you pay cash or take out a mortgage? What have you budgeted for maintenance and repair costs? If you are renting your home for part of the year, keep in mind that short-term renters don't often care for the home the way you would. What assumptions have you made about rental income, a property management company, taxes on the rental income, depreciation (which needs to be recaptured on your tax return when you sell the property), updates to your estate plan if you own out-of-state property, extra accounting fees, furnishings, dishes, sheets, towels, and other lifestyle needs for the home? Some of these up-front fees won't be annual expenses, but just because you buy a new mattress for each guest bedroom the first year doesn't mean you don't need to replace them every few years going forward. I have rarely seen people make out like bandits on rental property income once they truly account for all the expenses, both predictable and unpredictable.

Next, if you are looking to buy a second property because it's on sale, ask yourself some questions: Why is it on sale? Why is the owner trying to unload this property on the cheap? What did they pay for it—and what amount of loss are they about to incur? What has the trend been in home values in the area over the past three, five, ten years? Some people look the other way when doing their research because they don't want to know the hard truth that others aren't finding this beloved destination as attractive as it once used to be. They might get too caught up on the potential, in their minds, that they overlook the historical trend.

If you need to take money out of retirement savings early to buy this retirement dream home, you are forfeiting potential future growth on your liquid money. Remember, you can't buy groceries in retirement with the equity in your home(s). While you may have a lot of equity tied up in your primary home, taking liquid cash or future cash savings and buying more real estate can really tip the scales unfavorably in your retirement income plan. Plus, having more equity in real estate can mean you'll have to work longer and/or save more money now, so you have a big enough liquid nest egg to live off of in retirement. Working longer may be a huge negative just for the pleasure of owning a vacation home. It seems counterintuitive to work longer and have less time to spend at your second home, doesn't it?

Along with the goal of making memories at a family retreat often comes disappointment. Consider your own circumstances first. How often are you personally able to get to this destination home? What is the cost involved—both time and money— to travel to it? How many days do you reasonably need to spend there to make it worthwhile? Are you living with a fixed number of vacation days each year? Can you even sacrifice one Saturday a month, leaving behind other responsibilities or local activities, to spend time at your vacation home? Now, think about your family and the above list of considerations. The farther away from being in the workforce you are, the easier it is to forget about the constraints that those working and raising a family have when it comes to their downtime. If you can't find a set time each week to get your children or grandchildren on the phone, how likely is it that you can all agree on the one or two weeks a year that everyone will travel to this family retreat? Or how many years consecutively could your family commit to now? What if your home is in the mountains but everyone else prefers going to the beach?

Next, many early retired clients find themselves being the ones who travel to see their children and grandchildren because they have more time and flexibility to do so. That's another reason having this second home may cause disappointment if you are not able to use it as much as you'd like—if it means spending less time with your family. Your children and grandchildren may move, and you're likely to want to move near them too. How far away are you now from your vacation home? While you can have the best-laid plans and know where you want to live, you simply don't know where your children and grandchildren will end up residing.

As people age, they may not physically be able to travel to their second homes. Another headache to consider is the burden of leaving a home to family members if they can't afford to maintain it. If nobody wants your vacation home, someone else will be forced to figure out how and when to sell it.

Finally, I love the phrase "rent the best, invest the rest." This means instead of plunking down a lot of cash to own a second home, take some extra money each year and vacation wherever you want, whenever you want! You will likely spend much less over your lifetime by doing this, and you will be able to see many more places in the world. Consider this example:

You buy a $500,000 vacation home now, or spend $25,000 a year for twenty years ($25,000 x 20 = $500,000) to vacation at different places. With annual vacations, you know what you are spending and nobody is going to ask you to replace the carpet in the beach condo you rented for a month. Your expenses are more controllable, and that brings immense peace of mind in retirement.

Now, with all of the above factors, you may still want to own more than one property in retirement. Everyone has different goals, and this may be one of your big ones! If you do want a second home, be sure to "over save" for this purchase and the expenses that go along with it—and be emotionally prepared to unload it if your plans or family dynamics change.

Money Mistake 3: Keeping Up with the Joneses

This is all about controlling your spending. Just because you make more money as the years go by doesn't mean you need to spend more money. The sooner in your adult life you start trying to have the biggest and the best of everything, or match what your peers have (size of house, taste in cars, budget for dining out, etc.), the harder it will be for you to change your spending habits if your income doesn't keep up with your peers. It's like trying to lose weight—the longer you let your weight creep up on you, the more discipline and time it takes to get back to your ideal weight. The same goes for spending.

There are usually a lot of emotional factors that drive people to overspend and let their financial situations get out of control. Sometimes it stems from childhood experiences. I remember one gentleman telling me years ago how his parents instilled in him the notion that it was OK to spend beyond your means if you worked really hard—meaning you deserve to be rewarded because you are a hard worker. His parents racked up piles of debt and lived beyond their means for years, and this gentleman was struggling to convince himself that lifestyle was wrong. He knew he was headed down the wrong path as his lifestyle was exceeding his income well into his thirties. This trend is hard to reverse once you've started down this slippery slope.

Women who grew up privileged tend to have a hard time adjusting when their adult lives don't match the luxuries they experienced as children. If you marry someone who doesn't have a high-paying job or a family trust fund to fall back on, it's up to you to make the extra money if you want to enjoy that higher standard of living you've been accustomed to. There can be a lot of tension in a marriage if each spouse has a different definition of "comfortable lifestyle."

If you go through a divorce, it can be emotionally devastating if and when you realize you can't afford to raise your children in the same house, based on your alimony and/or child support payments. I've seen women put on the figurative earmuffs when I tell them they can't take the same types of vacations they used to or spend as much on gifts for their children as when they were married. When your personal financial circumstances change, don't bury your head in the sand by thinking nothing else in your life has to change. It does.

Also, even if keeping up with the Joneses was never important to you, as soon as you move into a more expensive neighborhood, you're throwing yourself in that situation. Usually with big houses come fancy cars, lush landscaping, and expensive social gatherings. Many children in these neighborhoods attend private schools. One thing can lead to the next, and suddenly you are needing to keep up with the Joneses so you can fit into the environment you chose.

I have yet to see a person or a couple successfully cut back their lifestyle more than a mediocre amount and stick with that new lifestyle. It's just so hard to do emotionally and financially. The best advice I can give to avoid Money Mistake 3 is to keep your spending in check early and often. Don't spend all the extra money you make each year. It's fine to treat yourself once in a while, but be aware of big lifestyle purchases that are not one-time expenses; otherwise, the family experiences you are having could easily become a pattern. For example, if you take one family vacation to Aruba this year, and next year it's Hawaii, will camping be acceptable the following year?

CHAPTER 8

I No Longer Do. Getting Divorced and Starting Over

Watching women come out of the divorce process scorned and bitter—and totally paralyzed from making any decisions with their money—is one of the main reasons I decided to author my first book in this Girl Talk, Money Talk series. I began my book series by educating women in their twenties and thirties about life's financial foundation messages. I'm now building on that with life experiences of women in their forties and fifties—and divorce is one of them.

At first, it was frustrating to me, a woman in finance, to see so many women come through my office door for the first time, after a divorce, exhibiting similar attitudes when it came to their money. They were scared to make decisions or take any small piece of advice; they worried it would be the wrong move and they'd end up homeless. They had lost a lot of trust in humanity going through the divorce process, yet when it comes to your money, if you are seeking advice, you must be able to trust the person giving you counsel.

I realize building trust takes time, but in the world of financial advising, trust is a two-way street. Advisers have to earn your trust and respect and prove they have your best interests at heart. Advisers must know you are capable of trusting them so you can move the relationship forward and implement their advice. If taking some time to educate yourself a little before walking into an adviser's office will calm your nerves, by all means, invest in yourself first!

Resetting your Financial Baseline

Once your divorce is finalized, you need to establish your new financial baseline. Where do you stand today with your assets, debts, income, and expenses? How will this change in the coming years if alimony and/or child support are part of your settlement? Two key financial statements you want to develop are your net worth (listing assets minus debts) and a multiyear cash flow projection showing income minus expenses.

As you look at your net worth statement, draw a pie chart to show how much of your money is in cash savings, retirement accounts, non-retirement investment accounts, business assets, real estate, and other assets. Is one piece of the pie chart exceedingly large or small? Those may be the areas that need your attention first. For example, if half of your pie chart is in real estate and only 10 percent is in retirement accounts such as an IRA, you'll want to focus on increasing your liquid savings for retirement.

Next, evaluate your debts. What is a good debt versus a bad debt? Good debt can be a mortgage or home equity line of credit or student loans, and bad debt is credit cards. You need a plan to pay off all your debts, especially before you retire. If you were not working a paid job before your divorce, and you find yourself saddled with debt now, you likely need to get a job to have extra money to pay off these debts.

Review your multiyear cash flow projection. Factoring in your income (alimony, child support, salary from a job or business), does that exceed your living expenses and taxes? How much is left over for savings? As I mentioned earlier, you really should make saving your priority before spending, but I understand most people don't view it that way. If you put this cash flow projection together and find a negative number on the bottom line—meaning your expenses are higher than your income—you need to get a job or a higher-paying job. Of course, you can plan to lower your standard of living to reduce your living expenses, but in my experience, that is very hard for people to do, especially overnight. For many people, spending less and making more are both necessary to stay on track financially.

Updating Other Areas of Your Financial Life

There are several financial and legal documents and personal items that need to be modified once your divorce is finalized. These include:

- your will, any trusts, health care power of attorney, and financial power of attorney;
- beneficiary designations on life insurance policies and retirement accounts;
- title of the house and car, bank accounts, joint investment accounts, and any other property that is changing ownership;
- your name change with Social Security, passport document, and driver's license;
- utility bills;
- the tax return (filing single or head of household versus married);
- your team of financial and legal advisers;
- children's school forms and contact information;
- passwords to your social media, financial accounts, or any other areas your ex-spouse may know how to access; and
- locks on doors and locations of extra keys.

Regarding your team of financial and legal advisers, going through your divorce may have brought you closer to one of your existing advisers—or you might feel more distanced from them. It's common for a married couple to work with separate financial and legal advisers during their divorce proceedings, as well as afterward. You want to ensure the people you hire post-divorce are only on your side and can think clearly about what is in your best interest going forward.

You also need to consider who will be your backup plan should you get sick, become disabled, or pass away. Someone needs to know how to access your financial and personal records, where safe-deposit boxes are located, how to access them, and who will be in charge of your household if you are unable to. While you'll name an executor in your will and agent(s) for your financial and health care matters in your legal documents, it's important for those agents to understand what you need them to do, what your expectations are, and if they are up to the task. Having a team of financial and legal advisers that can assist your trusted agent(s) to work through their responsibilities can be extremely valuable.

Making Big Changes

Your finances will change after going through a divorce—and so will your personal life. There will probably be a lot of personal disruptions. However, as tempting as it is to radically change your life and start everything new, now is not the time to make a big decision like selling your house and moving out of state, taking your kids out of private school, or dumping your BMW for a Ford. Now is the time to communicate with family members, run your numbers, get a sense of reality about what your options are going forward, and what changes, if any, you need to make to live comfortably and happy. Make methodical changes over time so you have time to ease into your adjusted situation.

Perhaps sacrifices need to be made—make a list of them. Factor in who will be impacted—is it you or you and your children? I've found many women don't want their children to have less, or feel they can't have it all, if the children were used to having it all before the divorce. Yet in order to keep the kids sheltered from the new reality, women can make poor money decisions that will hurt everyone in the long run. If your children are old enough, be open and honest with them about what changes you are going to make and why. Stand confidently on your own two feet when communicating this and show your children the power of resiliency, the power of self-confidence, and the power of taking action. You may find your relationship with your children will be better than before your divorce.

Monitor How Well You Are Doing

Once you have determined the changes you're going to make coming through your divorce, give yourself permission to reevaluate periodically. Take your temperature every three months at first and then move to a six-month evaluation cycle. How are you feeling about the decisions you've made? What financial and legal documents still need to be updated? Is life better than you expected? You may be pleasantly surprised by how well time heals wounds and how proud you'll feel of the progress you've made.

When you make a change, it can feel natural to decide two days later it's not going to work and reverse course, but that's rarely a way to make progress in life. Make sure you aren't making changes to your finances when you are highly emotional; that can be devastating. When it comes to your finances, changing your mind often on your strategy is never a good idea. With money, you need to have patience and give your strategy time to work. For example, you put a budget together and determine you have an extra $1,000 per month. You decide to put $500 toward retirement savings and $500 toward paying down your mortgage. Three months into your new plan, the stock market has been skyrocketing—and your retirement accounts are thriving. You might be tempted to put the entire $1,000 into retirement savings because it keeps going up! However, don't be surprised if the stock market goes down over the next three months—and now the guaranteed return you get by saving interest expense on your mortgage turns out to look better. Allow your financial strategy a full year before you reevaluate and determine whether to make any adjustments. For most people, having a savings and debt plan and sticking to that plan for multiple years will produce fruitful results. After a while, you will get so used to your savings and debt plan that you won't feel the urge to watch it closely. You will see the progress you've made, you will be happy with it, and you will experience the benefits of following a plan.

Getting Remarried

When you got married for the first time, you and your spouse likely didn't have much money. There wasn't much at risk financially or emotionally at that stage in your life. However, the playing field is different now. If you have been divorced and are thinking about getting married again, there are several financial factors to consider.

A priority should be finding the right time to openly discuss personal finances. The stakes are higher the second time around. You need to protect what you have—and you need to understand what your future spouse's financial situation looks like. Are you marrying a spendthrift? Is his/her balance sheet riddled with credit card debt? Are there alimony and child support payments lingering from a prior divorce? How much of your monthly joint expenses are you expected to cover versus your new spouse? Whose house will you live in? Will you be purchasing a new one?

If you have any concerns that your future spouse is not divulging all their financial details with you, keep asking. If your gut tells you there is a cover-up, that is a huge red flag for entering the marriage. Regardless, it is probably a wise idea for both of you to hire separate lawyers and draw up a prenuptial agreement to ensure you keep what you have—and you know what you'll be getting if the marriage does not work. While almost everyone wants to marry for love and not money, it's money that often leads couples down the road to divorce.

If you do get remarried, you'll need to run back through the above list, "Updating Other Areas of Your Financial Life," as your financial and legal affairs need to be updated again, including a new will, changes to insurance and beneficiary designations, and who will be in charge of your affairs if something happens to you.

At this point in your life, you have the experience of managing your own financial affairs. You likely know so much more about money than ever before. I encourage you to not let that slide even if you get remarried and your new spouse likes managing the household finances. Stay on top of your financial life, be an equal partner in the conversation, and remember this statistic, which could impact you again down the road: "At some point in their lives, due to divorce or death of a spouse, statistics show 90 percent of women will be solely responsible for their finances."[1]

Chapter Endnote:

1. Wall Street Journal. "Clients from Venus". 2012. https://www.wsj.com/articles/ SB10001424052970204190504577040402069714264.

CHAPTER 9

Tragedy Strikes. Losing Your Spouse or Partner

I hope you don't experience the loss of a spouse or partner for many years, but it's a reality many of us will face one day.

This emotionally devastating life event is where, as a financial adviser, I've seen the wheels fall off the bus for many women. I have sat across the table from women who were suddenly single due to the death of a spouse, and they were totally overwhelmed with the concept of money.

While it can feel premature to plan for the eventual death of your spouse or partner at this point in your life, it's not. Tomorrow is not guaranteed to anyone. As each year passes, you probably will know more and more people who die young from cancer, heart disease, or car accidents. If you are married or in a long-term relationship, it's never too soon to plan for the loss of your spouse or partner.

Depending upon who controls the finances in your household, it's important they don't keep it a secret. Even if you or your spouse or partner seems uninterested in this facet of life, you need to make it an annual priority to sit down and go through the household's financial details. Ensure you each know what assets, debts, income and expenses you have, how to access this information, and who to call for help. I've seen many people say the main reason they've hired a financial adviser is to make sure their spouse and family are taken care of if something happens to them (the one with the financial knowledge in the family). Even if you have an adviser, you still need to educate yourself on the what, how, and who points I just mentioned. If something happens to your spouse, you need direction on how to get organized and move forward with the finances.

One of the largest gaps in a person's financial affairs when they are in their forties and fifties is their estate plan. I know numerous individuals and couples in this age bracket who don't have a will, or if they have one, it's outdated and no longer fits their family's situation. If you are in this camp too, meet with a lawyer together and get your will, financial power of attorney, and health care directive updated immediately. If you don't have a will or it's in bad shape, this could cost thousands of dollars of wasted legal fees, taxes, hours as well as headaches for your loved ones to sort through after you are gone.

If you are single, the person named in your will as the executor needs to know the above what, how, and who points. What do you have? How do they access it if you are not around? Who do they call for help? Settling an estate is not easy—no matter how well organized you are. There will always be questions for your executor to find answers to, and having to deal with money stress while they are grieving can make matters worse. Have an annual conversation with the person or people who will be in charge of your estate if something happens to you. Provide them documentation in a sealed envelope annually—sort of like a "break glass in the event of an emergency" envelope.

What You Need to Know Now

Here are some near-term items to wrap your arms around now, in the event your spouse or partner does pass away prematurely:

- List of assets, debts, income and expenses
- How to access this information (paper statements, online access with user names and passwords)
- Last year's tax return
- Bill-pay service
- Life insurance and disability insurance policies
- Health insurance benefits and how this will change if they pass away
- Where to locate the will and other legal documents
- Social Security benefits information
- Contact information for all advisers such as financial, insurance agent, lawyer, tax accountant

Questions to Ask

- What should the family's financial priorities be in the event your spouse/partner passes away? Pay off the mortgage? Sell the business? Top off the college savings accounts? It's good to know what your spouse/partner would advise, what goals they find most important to achieve, and what risks they want you to avoid.

- What assets, debts, income, or expenses will not exist if your spouse or partner passes away?

This last question is incredibly important. Don't assume that you will inherit all of your spouse or partner's assets when they pass away. If they die without a will, the state you reside in could dictate what you get—and it's not always 100 percent. For any retirement accounts or life insurance policies your spouse or partner owns, the person(s) listed on the beneficiary form will inherit the money; it doesn't pass according to the will. If you are in a second marriage, and a former spouse is still listed as the life insurance beneficiary, you'll be out of luck. Understand how much life insurance you will receive, confirm you are listed as the beneficiary, and calculate whether this insurance plus other assets you'll inherit will be enough for you to maintain the standard of living you are accustomed to. Will you need to get a new job, downsize the home, take the children out of private school, or sell the beach house? If you don't know the answers to these questions, figure them out now and double-check the status annually to give yourself peace of mind and manage your expectations. It's certainly hard enough grieving the loss of the love of your life, but if you throw money stress and anxiety into the picture, you can quickly get overwhelmed or depressed.

If you have young children, I typically recommend having some life insurance on each spouse even if one doesn't work outside the home. There could be a caregiving cost to consider if the non-employed spouse passes away. What would childcare or a nanny cost in your area? How many years would this be required? If your spouse is a full-time parent, you need a lot of life insurance on your life.

Moving On after a Death

Even with a great financial plan in place before a loved one dies, it's natural to still feel anxious about moving on with your financial life. Don't rush into making any major decisions if you hadn't previously discussed them. For example, if you had planned enough life insurance so you wouldn't have to move out of your house until your youngest child graduated high school, don't panic and decide you need to sell the house now. If your spouse owned a business that has a great team of people running it now, maybe you can give it a few years before deciding to sell it—or even sell it to the new group of people who are taking over the day-to-day controls. If your plans did call for having to get a second job or going back to work, hopefully you have enough cash to be patient and find the right job for you, balancing all the other single-person and single-parent responsibilities.

Eventually, you need to move forward with your new financial life. There are some administrative items to address within the first year after your spouse or partner passes away.

First, assets and debts need to be re-titled into your name alone, not jointly held, including bank and investment accounts and real estate. You can work with a lawyer or financial adviser to help get this accomplished. Beneficiary designations on retirement accounts and life insurance you still own need to be updated, as does your will and other legal documents. Retirement accounts that you inherited will need to be rolled over to a spousal IRA or an inherited IRA. Typically, an inherited IRA is best for a spouse who is under age fifty-nine and a half and believes they will need to spend some of this money before they reach age fifty-nine and a half. That's because a 10 percent early withdrawal tax penalty would apply to spousal IRA withdrawals before age fifty-nine and a half— but not to withdrawals from an inherited IRA.

Bills will need to be in your name too. Keep track of what comes in the mail with your spouse or partner's name still on it and set those envelopes aside to determine whether any action is needed. This process will take time, and there will likely be a lot of forms to fill out, but you'll get there.

One piece of advice I've heard many times is it can take a year or more to settle someone's estate, and while I get raised eyebrows when I communicate this to clients, they most often shake their heads in agreement after that one-year period is up.

I understand getting all the administrative items behind you is part of the healing process—and you're going to want to ignore them at first—but keep a pile aside for when you are ready to address them.

CHAPTER 10

Top Ten Financial Moves

Here is a ten-step quick guide to get your money on track now. Use these tips to be proactive with your finances in your forties and fifties and prepare for a lifetime of success.

1. If you don't have basic knowledge about managing money, or you are not the one controlling the finances in your household, educate yourself now. Start with paying the bills and understanding every number on your tax return.

2. Your spending and savings formula should be: Income – Taxes – Savings = Expenses. If Savings comes last in your equation, rework your budget.

3. Save money based on your financial timeline of personal goals. Socking away money for retirement should be your most important goal—even if it's last on your timeline.

4. Cash and CDs are better investments for your emergency fund and short-term savings goals. Stocks, bonds, real estate, and other illiquid investments are better for long-term savings goals.

5. Never sabotage your long-term savings by panicking when a financial crisis hits.

6. Plan for the financial unexpected when times are good. Life will throw you curveballs, but with enough money in the bank, you can weather the storm.

7. Keep your lifestyle in check when you get a raise. Have a plan to save your new salary and bigger bonus—and don't buy the fancier car. Find a mentor and get involved with charity as you climb the corporate ladder.

8. If you plan to give up your career early, make sure you have enough savings or can live on one income. Know what sacrifices you need to make for your plan to work. The longer you are out of the workforce, the greater the impact on your financial future.

9. Steer clear of the three big money mistakes: the big house, the second house, and keeping up with the Joneses.

10. Divorce and premature death happen. Be prepared, know your family finances, pick your head up, and reset your financial baseline.

ABOUT THE AUTHOR

Lisa Brown is a partner in a wealth management firm located in Atlanta, Georgia, specializing in high-net-worth clients. Although Brown's clients are affluent, her own upbringing was far more modest. Raised by two schoolteachers in a rural farming town in upstate New York, Brown learned at the age of twelve how hard work translated into money, rising at six o'clock in the morning during her summer breaks to pick strawberries on a farm for twenty-five cents per quart. This perspective laid the foundation for the appreciation she has for money today.

Brown's childhood experience is at the opposite end of the financial spectrum from her professional experience. Over the years, she has been alarmed and frustrated by the number of single women approaching her for financial advice who shared the same unsettling characteristic: a lack of self-confidence when it came to making money decisions. These women have relied on their fathers, husbands, or partners to handle money matters throughout their lives, taking a back seat to this critical part of their world, and then suddenly found themselves on their own. Scared.

Lisa has taken two decades of experience in the financial services business to teach real-life money lessons to women in her Girl Talk, Money Talk book series. Her motivation is to educate women at an earlier age to take control of their finances, be prepared, and make wise decisions with their money that will have a profound effect on their entire lives.

Brown's financial advice has been featured in the *New York Times*, the *Wall Street Journal*, *CNBC.com*, and *Yahoo! Finance*, and she is a regular columnist for *Kiplinger's* wealth-creation website. In 2015, Brown was named one of the ten young advisers under the age of forty to watch by *Financial Advisor* magazine. She lives in the suburbs of Atlanta with her husband, three children, and Corgi.

Printed in the United States
by Baker & Taylor Publisher Services